JOHN
CALVIN

BOOKS BY JOHN PIPER

JOHN CALVIN

*and His Passion for the
Majesty of God*

JOHN PIPER

ivp

INTER-VARSITY PRESS
Norton Street, Nottingham NG7 3HR, England
Email: ivp@ivpbooks.com
Website: www.ivpbooks.com

Originally published in *The Legacy of Sovereign Joy: God's Triumphant Grace in the Lives of Augustine, Luther, and Calvin*, 2000.

First published 2009

British Library Cataloguing in Publication Data
A catalogue record for this book is available from the British Library.

ISBN 978-1-84474-356-8

Printed and bound in Great Britain by Ashford Colour Press Ltd, Gosport, Hampshire

Inter-Varsity Press publishes Christian books that are true to the Bible and that communicate the gospel, develop discipleship and strengthen the church for its mission in the world.

Inter-Varsity Press is closely linked with the Universities and Colleges Christian Fellowship, a student movement connecting Christian Unions in universities and colleges throughout Great Britain, and a member movement of the International Fellowship of Evangelical Students. Website: www.uccf.org.uk

CONTENTS

FOREWORD

The year 2009 marks the five-hundredth anniversary of the birth of John Calvin, by common consent one of the greatest, but also one of the most controversial, Christian leaders who ever lived. Yet for a man who stood at the center of the revolutionary upheavals of sixteenth-century Europe and who was personally involved in trying to reform churches from Scotland to Hungary, Calvin is surprisingly little known.

People write plays and make films about Martin Luther but not about John Calvin, who seems much harder to pin down. We know very little about his early life and almost nothing about his conversion, which must have happened sometime in 1533 or 1534. His wanderings over the next several years, including his extended stay with Martin Bucer in Strasbourg, are better documented, but despite the adventures his travels entailed, they have never seemed to be the stuff of high drama.

The Geneva years are the best known, but even they are widely misunderstood. Few people realize that Calvin was a foreigner in Geneva who was not granted citizenship there until 1559, and so he could never take part in the city's government. Even fewer realize that Calvin's Geneva was not a theocracy but a worldly city-state with which he was frequently at odds. Never a well man, there were times when he almost had to be dragged out of his sickbed to preach from the pulpit of the main city church, and it was something of a miracle that he lived as long as he did.

Yet today more people read Calvin's writings than those of any other Christian outside the New Testament writers. His commentaries remain standard works in and are generally regarded as the first great monument of modern biblical scholarship. His *Institutes of the Christian Religion* are still required reading for any serious theologian. Even some of his sermons are still in print, though they are unfortunately less well known than his other writings, and many remain in nearly undecipherable manuscript in Geneva, while many more have been lost because the manuscripts were sold for scrap a couple of centuries ago.

Calvin was not an original thinker in the sense that Martin Luther or Erasmus of Rotterdam were. He did not discover any new theological principle to set the church on fire, as Luther did. He did not recover any secrets of ancient wisdom as Erasmus was known for doing. His lifelong ambition was to see the conversion of France to Protestantism, but although he was able to gather French Protestants under his wing, they failed to take over France, and Calvin had to be content with England and Scotland instead—Holland did not accept his teachings until after his death. Calvin was great, not for his originality or for his achievements, but for his deep grasp of the coherence of the Christian message, which stemmed from his profound relationship with God.

Calvin was a man possessed by the Holy Spirit. He knew that he had been called to meet with God in Christ and to spread God's Word to a hungry and dying world, and he never flagged in that mission. From the start, he understood that to know God is to step into another world, to be born again into a relationship with the One who made and governs all things, and who had called a people, who did not deserve it, to rule that creation at his side. He knew that this relationship had many facets to it, but he also understood its fundamental coherence, and it was this that he brought to his study and exposition of Christian theology.

Fundamental to that theology was the Word of God, the Old and New Testaments that together make up the Bible. Here the variety and inner coherence of God and his plan for his creatures was displayed to the full. Systematic theology was an exposition of that coherence, and in his sermons Calvin applied that understanding to the practical needs of the church. Everything hung together because there was only one God and one eternal mind at work, undergirding it all. It is this knowledge that gave Calvin's work its strength, and it was this that struck fear into the hearts of his enemies.

Men like Luther and Augustine have had devoted followers, but few have had as many equally dedicated enemies as Calvin has attracted over the years. He has never left people indifferent—either you follow him or you turn against his teaching. In that respect, he was uncannily like Jesus, who likewise left none of his hearers untouched one way or the other. If Calvin himself had realized this similarity, it would have pleased him more than anything in the world, because his only ambition was to take up his cross and follow his Lord.

Today the world has changed in many ways, but at bottom it remains the same as ever. The hearts of people, including many church people, are cold and led astray by an array of false gods. Material prosperity has dulled the spirits of many, and our civilization is drowning in intellectual trivia and moral turpitude, while at the same time it convinces itself that it is the highest form of life yet achieved by the human race. In this world, Calvin's voice needs to be heard again. God will not be mocked, and in the end we shall discover that he is our Sovereign Lord. What will he say to you on the day of judgment?

Calvin had no doubts about this—he knew that he would be welcomed into the joy of his Lord as a good and faithful servant. John Piper has brought that message to life for a new generation, and I hope and pray that this study of the great Reformer will stir the hearts of all who read it to seek God's face again and to turn to him and live.

Gerald Bray, Research Professor,
Beeson Divinity School, Samford University,
Birmingham, Alabama

GOD IS WHO HE IS

John Calvin would approve that we begin with God rather than with him. Nothing mattered more to Calvin than the supremacy of God over all things. Focus your attention, then, on God's self-identification in Exodus 3:14–15. Here we will see the sun in the solar system of John Calvin's thought and life.

God calls Moses and commissions him to go to Egypt and bring his people out of bondage. Moses is frightened at this prospect and raises the objection that he is not the person to do this. God responds by saying, "I will be with you" (Ex. 3:12). Then Moses says, "[When I] say to them, 'The God of your fathers has sent me to you,' and [when] they ask me, 'What is his name?' what shall I say to them?" (v. 13). God's response is one of the most important revelations that has ever been given to man:

> God said to Moses, "I AM WHO I AM." And he said, "Say this to the people of Israel, 'I AM has sent me to you.'" God also said to Moses, "Say this to the people of Israel, 'The LORD, the God of your fathers, the God of Abraham, the God of Isaac, and the God of Jacob, has sent me to you.' This is my name forever, and thus I am to be remembered throughout all generations. (vv. 14–15)

In other words, the great, central, biblical name of *Yahweh* is explicitly rooted by God himself in the phrase "I AM WHO I AM." "Tell them, *the one who simply and absolutely is* has sent you. Tell them that the essential thing about me is that I am."

A Passion for the Centrality and Supremacy of God

I begin with this biblical self-identification of God because the unhidden and unashamed aim in this book is to fan the flame of your passion for the centrality and supremacy of God. Does not our heart burn when we hear God say, "My name is, 'I AM WHO I AM'"? The absoluteness of God's existence enthralls the mind: God's never beginning, never ending, never becoming, never improving, simply and absolutely there—to be dealt with on his terms or not at all.

Let this sink in: God—the God who holds you in being this very moment—never had a beginning. Ponder it. Do you remember the first time you thought about this as a child or young teenager? Let that speechless wonder rise. God never had a beginning! "I AM" has sent me to you. And one who never had a beginning, but always was and is and will be, defines all things. Whether we want him to be there or not, he is there. We do not negotiate what we want for reality. *God* defines reality. When we come into existence, we stand before a God who made us and owns us. We have absolutely no choice in this matter. We do not choose to be. And when we are, we do not choose that God be. No ranting and raving, no sophisticated doubt or skepticism, has any effect on the existence of God. He simply and absolutely is. "Tell them 'I AM' has sent you."

If we don't like it, we can change, to our joy, or we can resist, to our destruction. But one thing remains absolutely unassailed: God *is*. He was there before we came. He will be there after we are gone. And therefore what matters in life above all things is this God. We cannot escape the simple and obvious truth that God must be the main thing in life. Life has to do with God because all the universe has to do with God, and the universe has to do with God because every atom and every emotion and every soul of every angelic, demonic, and human being belongs to God, who absolutely *is*. He created all that is, he sustains everything in being, he directs the course of all events, because "from him and through him and to him are all things. To him be glory forever" (Rom. 11:36).

A Passion for the Majesty of God

May God inflame in you a passion for his centrality and supremacy in your life. May it be so that when you are dead and gone the people you love and serve will say, "This one knew God. This one loved God and lived for the glory of God and showed us God day after day. This one, as the apostle said, was 'filled with all the fullness of God'" (Eph. 3:19).

This is the aim and the burden of this book. Not only because the majesty of God is *im*plicit in the sheer, awesome existence of God, and not only because it is *ex*plicit in the Word of God, but also because David Wells is staggeringly right when he says, "It is this God, majestic and holy in his being . . . who has disappeared from the modern evangelical world."[1] Lesslie Newbigin says much the same thing: "I suddenly saw that someone could use all the language of evangelical Christianity, and yet the center was fundamentally the self, my need of salvation. And God is auxiliary to that. . . . I also saw that quite a lot of evangelical Christianity can easily slip, can become centered in me and my need of salvation, and not in the glory of God."[2] And, oh, have we slipped. Where are the churches today where the dominant experience is the precious weight of the glory of God? May God restore a passion for his majesty in our day.

---

[1]David Wells, *No Place for Truth* (Grand Rapids, MI: Eerdmans, 1993), 300.
[2]Quoted in Tim Stafford, "God's Missionary to Us," *Christianity Today*, December 9, 1996, 29.

CHAPTER TWO

A PASSION FOR THE GLORY OF GOD IN CHRIST

God rests lightly on the church in our time, and John Calvin saw the same thing in his own day.

In 1538, the Italian Cardinal Sadolet wrote to the leaders of Geneva trying to win them back to the Roman Catholic Church after they had turned to the Reformed teachings. He began his letter with a long conciliatory section on the preciousness of eternal life, before coming to his accusations of the Reformation. Calvin wrote the response to Sadolet in six days in the fall of 1539. It was one of his earliest writings and spread his name as a reformer across Europe. Luther read it and said, "Here is a writing which has hands and feet. I rejoice that God raises up such men."[1]

Calvin's Unremitting Zeal to Illustrate the Glory of God

Calvin's response to Sadolet is important because it uncovers the root of Calvin's quarrel with Rome, which would determine his whole life. The issue is not, first, the well-known sticking points of the Reformation: justification,

[1]Henry F. Henderson, *Calvin in His Letters* (London: J. M. Dent, 1909), 68.

priestly abuses, transubstantiation, prayers to saints, and papal authority. All those will come in for discussion. But beneath all of them, the fundamental issue for John Calvin—from the beginning of his life to the end—was the issue of *the centrality and supremacy and majesty of the glory of God*. He saw in Sadolet's letter the same thing Newbigin sees in self-saturated evangelicalism.[2]

Here's what Calvin said to the Cardinal: "[Your] zeal for heavenly life [is] a zeal which keeps a man entirely devoted to himself, and does not, even by one expression, arouse him to *sanctify the name of God*." In other words, even precious truth about eternal life can be so skewed as to displace God as the center and goal. This was Calvin's chief contention with Rome, and it comes out in his writings over and over again. He goes on and says to Sadolet that what he should do—and what Calvin aims to do with all his life—is "set before [man], as the prime motive of his existence, *zeal to illustrate the glory of God*."[3]

I think this would be a fitting banner over all of John Calvin's life and work—zeal to illustrate the glory of God. The essential meaning of John Calvin's life and preaching is that *he recovered and embodied a passion for the absolute reality and majesty of God*. That is what I want us to see most clearly. Benjamin Warfield said of Calvin, "No man

---

[2]Quoted in Tim Stafford, "God's Missionary to Us," *Christianity Today,* December 9, 1996, 29.
[3]John Dillenberger, *John Calvin, Selections from His Writings* (Atlanta: Scholars Press, 1975), 89; emphasis added.

ever had a profounder sense of God than he."[4] There's the key to Calvin's life and theology.

Geerhardus Vos, the Princeton New Testament scholar, asked this question in 1891: Why has Reformed theology been able to grasp the fullness of Scripture unlike any other branch of Christendom? He answered, "Because Reformed theology took hold of the Scriptures in their deepest root idea. . . . This root idea which served as the key to unlock the rich treasuries of the Scriptures was *the preeminence of God's glory in the consideration of all that has been created.*"[5] It is this relentless orientation toward the glory of God that gives coherence to John Calvin's life and to the Reformed tradition that followed. Vos said that the "all-embracing slogan of the Reformed faith is this: the work of grace in the sinner is a *mirror for the glory of God.*"[6] Mirroring the glory of God is the meaning of John Calvin's life and ministry.

When Calvin did eventually get to the issue of justification in his response to Sadolet, he said, "You . . . touch upon justification by faith, the first and keenest subject of controversy between us. . . . Wherever the knowledge of it is taken away, *the glory of Christ is extinguished.*"[7] So here again we can see what is fundamental. Justification by faith is crucial. But there is a deeper reason why it is crucial. The glory of Christ is at stake. Wherever the knowledge of jus-

---

[4]Benjamin Warfield, *Calvin and Augustine* (Philadelphia: Presbyterian and Reformed, 1971), 24.
[5]Geerhardus Vos, "The Doctrine of the Covenant in Reformed Theology," in *Redemptive History and Biblical Interpretation: The Shorter Writings of Geerhardus Vos* (Phillipsburg, NJ: Presbyterian and Reformed, 1980), 241–42; emphasis added.
[6]Ibid., 248; emphasis added.
[7]Dillenberger, *John Calvin*, 95; emphasis added.

tification is taken away, the glory of Christ is extinguished. This is always the deepest issue for Calvin. What truth and what behavior will "illustrate the glory of God"?

Moved by a Passion to Display God's Glory

For Calvin, the need for the Reformation was fundamentally this: Rome had "destroyed the glory of Christ in many ways—by calling upon the saints to intercede, when Jesus Christ is the one mediator between God and man; by adoring the Blessed Virgin, when Christ alone shall be adored; by offering a continual sacrifice in the Mass, when the sacrifice of Christ upon the Cross is complete and sufficient,"[8] by elevating tradition to the level of Scripture and even making the word of Christ dependent for its authority on the word of man.[9] Calvin asks, in his *Commentary on Colossians*, "How comes it that we are 'carried about with so many strange doctrines' (Hebrews 13:9)?" He answers, "Because the excellence of Christ is not perceived by us."[10] In other words, the great guardian of biblical orthodoxy throughout the centuries is a passion for the glory and the excellency of God in Christ. Where the center shifts from God, everything begins to shift everywhere—a fact which does not bode well for doctrinal faithfulness in our own non-God-centered day.

---

[8]T. H. L. Parker, *Portrait of Calvin* (Philadelphia: Westminster Press, 1954), 109.

[9]John Calvin, *Institutes of the Christian Religion*, bk. 1, chap., 7, 1. "A most pernicious error widely prevails that Scripture has only so much weight as is conceded to it by the consent of the church. As if the eternal and inviolable truth of God depended upon the decision of men!" John Calvin, *Institutes of the Christian religion*, ed. John Thomas McNeill and Ford Lewis Battles, The Library of Christian Classics, vol. 21 (Philadelphia: Westminster Press, 1960).

[10]Parker, *Portrait of Calvin*, 55.

Therefore the unifying root of all of Calvin's labors is his passion to display the glory of God in Christ. When he was thirty years old, he described an imaginary scene of himself at the end of his life, giving an account to God. He said, "The thing [O God] at which I chiefly aimed, and for which I most diligently labored, was, that the glory of thy goodness and justice . . . might shine forth conspicuous, that the virtue and blessings of thy Christ . . . might be fully displayed."[11]

Twenty-four years later, unchanged in his passions and goals, and one month before he actually did give an account to Christ in heaven (he died at age fifty-four), he said in his last will and testament, "I have written nothing out of hatred to any one, but I have always faithfully propounded what I esteemed to be *for the glory of God.*"[12]

---

[11]Dillenberger, *John Calvin*, 110.
[12]Ibid., 42; emphasis added.

MASTERED BY THE MAJESTY AND WORD OF GOD

What happened to John Calvin to make him a man so mastered by the majesty of God? And what kind of ministry did this produce in his life?

He was born July 10, 1509, in Noyon, France, when Martin Luther was twenty-five years old and had just begun to teach the Bible in Wittenberg. We know almost nothing of Calvin's early home life. When he was fourteen, his father sent him to study theology at the University of Paris, which at that time was untouched by the Reformation and steeped in medieval theology. But five years later (when Calvin was nineteen) his father ran afoul of the church and told his son to leave theology and study law, which he did for the next three years at Orleans and Bourges.

During these years Calvin mastered Greek and was immersed in the thought of Duns Scotus, William Ockham, and Gabriel Biel, and he completed his law course. His father died in May of 1531, when Calvin was twenty-one. Calvin felt free then to turn from law to his first love, which had become the classics. He published his first book, a *Commentary on Seneca*, in 1532, at the age of twenty-three.

But sometime during these years he came into contact with the message and the spirit of the Reformation, and by 1533 something dramatic had happened in his life.

Calvin's Conversion

In November of 1533, Nicholas Cop, a friend of Calvin, preached at the opening of the winter term at the University of Paris and was called to account by the Parliament for his Lutheran-like doctrines. He fled the city, and a general persecution broke out against what King Francis I called "the cursed Lutheran sect." Calvin was among those who escaped. The connection with Cop was so close that some suspect Calvin actually wrote the message that Cop delivered. So by 1533 Calvin had crossed the line. He was now wholly devoted to the cause of the Reformation.

What had happened? Calvin recounts, seven years later, how his conversion came about. He describes how he had been struggling to live out the Catholic faith with zeal,

> . . . when, lo, a very different form of doctrine started up, not one which led us away from the Christian profession, but one which brought it back to its fountain . . . to its original purity. Offended by the novelty, I lent an unwilling ear, and at first, I confess, strenuously and passionately resisted . . . to confess that I had all my life long been in ignorance and error. . . .
>
> I at length perceived, as if light had broken in upon me [a very key phrase, in view of what we will see], in what a sty of error I had wallowed, and how much pollution

and impurity I had thereby contracted. Being exceedingly alarmed at the misery into which I had fallen . . . as in duty bound, [I] made it my first business to betake myself to thy way [O God], condemning my past life, not without groans and tears.[1]

God, by a sudden conversion subdued and brought my mind to a teachable frame. . . . Having thus received some taste and knowledge of true godliness, I was immediately inflamed with [an] intense desire to make progress.[2]

What was the foundation of Calvin's faith that yielded a life devoted utterly to displaying the glory and majesty of God? The answer seems to be that Calvin suddenly, as he says, saw and tasted in Scripture the majesty of God. And in that moment, both God and the Word of God were so powerfully and unquestionably authenticated to his soul that he became the loving servant of God and his Word the rest of his life. This experience and conviction dethroned the church as the authority that accredits the Scriptures for the saints. The majesty of God himself in the Word was sufficient for this work.[3]

---

[1]John Dillenberger, *John Calvin, Selections from His Writings* (Atlanta: Scholars Press, 1975), 114–15.

[2]Ibid., 26.

[3]Calvin, as he so often did, laid hold on Augustine to strengthen his claim that this was the historic position of the church, in spite of the Roman Catholic teaching that the church authorizes the Scriptures for the believer. Commenting on Augustine's view of the role of the authority of the church in leading to a well-founded faith in Scripture, Calvin wrote, "He only meant to indicate what we also confess as true: those who have not yet been illumined by the Spirit of God are rendered teachable by reverence for the church, so that they may persevere in learning faith in Christ from the gospel. Thus, he avers, the authority of the church is an introduction through which we are prepared for faith in the gospel. For, as we see, he wants the certainty of the godly to rest upon a far different foundation" (*Institutes of the Christian Religion*, 1.7.3).

The Majesty of God: Ground for Confidence in His Word

How this happened is extremely important, and we need to see how Calvin himself describes it in the *Institutes*, especially book 1, chapters 7 and 8. Here he wrestles with how we can come to a saving knowledge of God through the Scriptures. His answer is the famous phrase "the internal testimony of the Holy Spirit." For example, he says, "Scripture will ultimately suffice for a saving knowledge of God only when its certainty is founded upon the inward persuasion of the Holy Spirit" (I, viii, 13). So two things came together for Calvin to give him a "saving knowledge of God": Scripture and the "inward persuasion of the Holy Spirit." Neither alone suffices to save.

But how does this actually work? What does the Spirit do? The answer is not that the Spirit gives us added revelation to what is in Scripture,[4] but that he awakens us, as from the dead, to see and taste the divine reality of God in Scripture, which authenticates it as God's own Word. He says, "Our Heavenly Father, revealing his majesty [in Scripture], lifts reverence for Scripture beyond the realm of controversy" (I, viii, 13). There is the key for Calvin: the witness of God to Scripture is the immediate, unassailable,

---

[4] J. I. Packer, "Calvin the Theologian," in *Honouring the People of God: Collected Shorter Writings of J. I. Packer*, vol. 4 (Carlisle: Paternoster, 1999), 156. "Rejecting both the Roman contention that the Scripture is to be received as authoritative on the church's authority, and the idea that Scripture could be proved divinely authoritative by rational argument alone, Calvin affirms Scripture to be self-authenticating through the inner witness of the Holy Spirit. What is this 'inner witness'? Not a special quality of experience, nor a new, private revelation, nor an existential 'decision,' but a work of enlightenment whereby, through the medium of verbal testimony, the blind eyes of the spirit are opened, and divine realities come to be recognized and embraced for what they are."

life-giving revelation to our minds of *the majesty of God* that is manifest in the Scriptures themselves. The majesty of God is the ground of our confidence in his Word.

Over and over again in Calvin's description of what happens in coming to faith, you see his references to the majesty of God revealed in Scripture and vindicating Scripture. So already in the dynamics of his conversion, the central passion of his life is being ignited.

The Word Mediating the Majesty

We are almost at the bottom of this experience now. If we go just a bit deeper we will see more clearly why this conversion resulted in such an "invincible constancy" in Calvin's lifelong allegiance to the majesty of God and the truth of God's Word. Here are the words that will take us deeper:

> Therefore illumined by [the Spirit's] power, we believe neither by our own [note this!] nor by anyone else's judgment that Scripture is from God; but above human judgment we affirm with utter certainty (just as if we were gazing upon the majesty of God himself) that it has flowed to us from the very mouth of God by the ministry of men.[5]

This is almost baffling. He says that his conviction concerning the majesty of God in Scripture rests not on any human judgment—not even his own. What does he mean? Perhaps the words of the apostle John shed the most helpful

---

[5]Calvin, *Institutes* 1.7.5.

light on what Calvin is trying to explain. Here are the key words from 1 John 5:6–11:

> The Spirit is the one who testifies, because the Spirit is the truth. . . . If we receive the testimony of men, the testimony of God [the Spirit] is greater, for this is the testimony of God that he has borne concerning his Son. . . . And this is the testimony, that God gave us eternal life, and this life is in his Son.

In other words, the "testimony of God," that is, the inward witness of the Spirit, is greater than any human witness—including, John would probably say in this context, the witness of our own judgment. And what is that witness of God? It is not merely a word delivered to our judgment for reflection, for then our conviction would rely on that reflection. What is it then? Verse 11 is the key: "This is the testimony, that God gave us eternal life." I take that to mean that God witnesses to us of his reality and the reality of his Son and his Word by giving us life from the dead so that we come alive. His witness is the gift of spiritual life. His witness is that we come alive to his majesty and see him for who he is in his Word. In that instant, we do not reason from premises to conclusions—we see that we are awake, and there is not even a prior human judgment about it to lean on. When Lazarus was awakened in the tomb by the call or the "testimony" of Christ, he knew without reasoning that he was alive and that this call had wakened him.

Here's the way J. I. Packer puts it:

[The internal witness of the Spirit in John Calvin] is a work of enlightenment whereby, through the medium of verbal testimony, the blind eyes of the spirit are opened, and divine realities come to be recognized and embraced for what they are. This recognition, Calvin says, is as immediate and unanalysable as the perceiving of a colour, or a taste, by physical sense—an event about which no more can be said than that when appropriate stimuli were present it happened, and when it happened we knew it had happened.[6]

Blind Eyes Opened

So in his early twenties John Calvin experienced the miracle of having the blind eyes of his spirit opened by the Spirit of God. And what he saw immediately, and without any intervening chain of human reasoning, were two things so interwoven that they would determine the rest of his life: the majesty of God and the Word of God. The Word mediated the majesty, and the majesty vindicated the Word. Henceforth he would be a man utterly devoted to displaying the majesty of God by the exposition of the Word of God.

---

[6]Packer, "Calvin the Theologian," 156.

MINISTRY MADE BY THE MAJESTY OF THE WORD

What form would Calvin's ministry take? He knew what he wanted. He wanted the enjoyment of literary ease so he could promote the Reformed faith as a literary scholar.[1] That is what he thought he was cut out for by nature. But God had radically different plans—as he had for Augustine and Luther—and for many of us who did not plan our lives the way they have turned out.

An Unexpected Ministry

After escaping from Paris and finally leaving France entirely, Calvin spent his exile in Basel, Switzerland, between 1534 and 1536. To redeem the time, "he devoted himself to the study of Hebrew."[2] (Imagine such a thing! Would any pastor today, exiled from his church and country, and living in mortal danger, study Hebrew? What has become of the vision of ministry that such a thing seems unthinkable today?) In March of 1536, he published the

[1]John Dillenberger, *John Calvin, Selections from His Writings* (Atlanta: Scholars Press, 1975), 86.
[2]Theodore Beza, *The Life of John Calvin* (Milwaukee, OR: Back Home Industries, 1996, from the 1844 Edinburgh edition of the Calvin Translation Society), 21.

first edition of his most famous work, *The Institutes of the Christian Religion*, which would go through five enlargements before reaching its present form in 1559. And we should not think that this was a merely academic exercise for Calvin. Years later he tells us what was driving him:

> But lo! while I lay hidden at Basel, and known only to few people, many faithful and holy persons were burnt alive in France. . . . It appeared to me, that unless I opposed [the perpetrators] to the utmost of my ability, my silence could not be vindicated from the charge of cowardice and treachery. This was the consideration which induced me to publish my *Institutes of the Christian Religion*. . . . It was published with no other design than that men might know what was the faith held by those whom I saw basely and wickedly defamed. [3]

Theology Forged in the Furnace of Martyrdom

So when you hold the *Institutes* of John Calvin in your hand, remember that theology, for John Calvin, was forged in the furnace of martyrdom, and that Calvin could not sit idly by without some effort to vindicate the faithful and the God for whom they suffered. I think we would, perhaps, do our theology better today if more were at stake in what we said.

In 1536, France gave a temporary amnesty to those who had fled. Calvin returned, put his things in order, and left, never to return, taking his brother Antoine and

---

[3]Dillenberger, *John Calvin*, 27.

sister Marie with him. He intended to go to Strasbourg and continue his life of peaceful literary production. But he wrote later to a friend, "I have learned from experience that we cannot see very far before us. When I promised myself an easy, tranquil life, what I least expected was at hand."[4] A war between Charles V and Francis I resulted in troop movements that blocked the road to Strasbourg, and Calvin had to detour through Geneva. In retrospect, one has to marvel at the providence of God that he should so arrange armies to position his pastors where he wanted them.

The night that Calvin stayed in Geneva, William Farel, the fiery leader of the Reformation in that city, found out he was there and sought him out. It was a meeting that changed the course of history—not just for Geneva, but for the world. In his preface to his commentary on Psalms Calvin tells us what happened:

> Farel, who burned with an extraordinary zeal to advance the gospel, immediately learned that my heart was set upon devoting myself to private studies, for which I wished to keep myself free from other pursuits, and finding that he gained nothing by entreaties, he proceeded to utter an imprecation that God would curse my retirement, and the tranquillity of the studies which I sought, if I should withdraw and refuse to give assistance, when the necessity was so urgent. By this imprecation I was so stricken with terror, that I desisted from the journey which I had undertaken.[5]

---

[4]T. H. L. Parker, *Portrait of Calvin* (Philadelphia: Westminster Press, 1954), 24.
[5]Dillenberger, *John Calvin*, 28.

The Anvil of Pastoral Responsibility

The course of his life was irrevocably changed—not just geographically, but vocationally. Never again would Calvin work in what he called the "tranquility of . . . studies." From then on, every page of the forty-eight volumes of books and tracts and sermons and commentaries and letters that he wrote would be hammered out on the anvil of pastoral responsibility.

He took up his responsibilities in Geneva first as professor of sacred Scripture, and within four months was appointed pastor of St. Peter's church—one of the three parishes in the ten-thousand-person town of Geneva. But the city council was not altogether happy, because Farel and Calvin did not bow to all their wishes. So the two of them were banished in April of 1538.

Calvin breathed a sigh of relief and thought God was relieving him from the crush of pastoral duties so that he could be about his studies. But when Martin Bucer found out about Calvin's availability, he did the same thing to get him to Strasbourg that Farel had done to get him to Geneva. Calvin wrote, "That most excellent servant of Christ, Martin Bucer, employing a similar kind of remonstrance and protestation as that to which Farel had recourse, before, drew me back to a new station. Alarmed by the example of Jonah which he set before me, I still continued in the work of teaching."[6] That is, he agreed to go to Strasbourg and teach. In fact,

---

[6]Ibid., 29.

for three years Calvin served as the pastor to about five hundred French refugees in Strasbourg, as well as teaching New Testament. He also wrote his first commentary, on Romans, and put out the second enlarged edition of the *Institutes*.

MARRIAGE TO IDELETTE

Perhaps the most important providence during this three-year stay in Strasbourg was finding a wife. Several had tried to find a wife for Calvin, who was thirty-one years old. Numerous women had shown interest. Calvin had told his friend and matchmaker William Farel what he wanted in a wife: "The only beauty which allures me is this—that she be chaste, not too nice or fastidious, economical, patient, likely to take care of my health."[1] Parker comments, "Romantic love . . . seems to have had no place in his character. Yet prosaic wooing led to a happy marriage."[2] I think Parker was wrong about romantic love (see below on Idelette's death).

An Anabaptist widow named Idelette Stordeur was the subject of John Calvin's "prosaic wooing." She and her husband, John, had joined Calvin's congregation. In the spring of 1540, John died of plague, and on August 6, 1540, Calvin and Idelette were married. She brought a son and daughter with her into Calvin's home.

Meanwhile, back in Geneva, chaos was making the city

---

[1] T. H. L. Parker, *Portrait of Calvin* (Philadelphia: Westminster Press, 1954), 70.
[2] Ibid., 69.

fathers think that maybe Calvin and Farel were not so bad after all. On May 1, 1541, the city council rescinded the ban on Calvin and even held him up as a man of God. This created an agonizing decision for Calvin, because he knew that life in Geneva would be full of controversy and danger. Earlier in October, he said to Farel that though he preferred not to go, "yet because I know that I am not my own master, I offer my heart as a true sacrifice to the Lord."[3] This became Calvin's motto, and the picture on his emblem included a hand holding out a heart to God with the inscription *prompte et sincere* ("promptly and sincerely").

Personal Sorrow

On Tuesday, September 13, 1541, Calvin entered Geneva for the second time to serve the church there until his death on May 27, 1564. His first son, Jacques, was born July 28, 1542, and died two weeks later. He wrote to his friend Viret, "The Lord has certainly inflicted a severe and bitter wound in the death of our baby son. But He is Himself a Father and knows best what is good for his children."[4] This is the kind of submission to the sovereign hand of God that Calvin rendered in all of his countless trials.

Idelette was never well again. They had two more children who also died at or soon after birth. Then on March 29, 1549, Idelette died of what was probably tuberculosis. Calvin wrote to Viret:

---

[3]W. de Greef, *The Writings of John Calvin: An Introductory Guide*, trans. Lyle D. Bierma (Grand Rapids, MI: Baker, 1993), 38.
[4]Parker, *Portrait of Calvin*, 71.

You know well how tender, or rather soft, my mind is. Had not a powerful self-control been given to me, I could not have borne up so long. And truly, mine is no common source of grief. I have been bereaved of the best companion of my life, of one who, had it been so ordained, would have willingly shared not only my poverty but even my death. During her life she was the faithful helper of my ministry. From her I never experienced the slightest hindrance. She was never troublesome to me throughout the whole course of her illness, but was more anxious about her children than about herself. As I feared these private worries might upset her to no purpose, I took occasion three days before she died, to mention that I would not fail in discharging my duty towards her children.[5]

---

[5]Ibid.

.

CHAPTER SIX

CONSTANT TRIALS

Calvin never remarried. And it is just as well. The pace he kept would not have left much time for wife or children. His acquaintance Nicolas Colladon, who lived in Geneva during these years, describes his life:

> Calvin for his part did not spare himself at all, working far beyond what his power and regard for his health could stand. He preached commonly every day for one week in two [and twice on every Sunday, or a total of about ten times every fortnight]. Every week he lectured three times in theology. . . . Every Friday at the Bible Study . . . what he added after the leader had made his *declaration* was almost a lecture. He never failed in visiting the sick, in private warning and counsel, and the rest of the numberless matters arising out of the ordinary exercise of his ministry. But besides these ordinary tasks, he had great care for believers in France, both in teaching them and exhorting and counseling them and consoling them by letters when they were being persecuted, and also in interceding for them. . . . Yet all that did not prevent him from going on working at his special study and composing many splendid and very useful books.[1]

---

[1]T. H. L. Parker, *Calvin's Preaching* (Louisville: Westminster,1992), 62–63.

Calvin's Perseverance

He was, as the Reformer Wolfgang Musculus called him, "a bow always strung." In one way, he tried to take heed to his health, but it probably did more harm than good. Colladon says that "he took little regard to his health, mostly being content for many years with a single meal a day and never taking anything between two meals." His reasons were that the weakness of his stomach and his migraines could only be controlled, he had found by experiment, by continual abstinence.[2]

Contrarily, Calvin was apparently careless of his health and worked night and day with scarcely a break. You can hear the drivenness in this letter to Falais in 1546: "Apart from the sermons and the lectures, there is a month gone by in which I have scarce done anything, in such wise I am almost ashamed to live thus useless"[3]—a mere twenty sermons and twelve lectures in that month!

To get a clearer picture of his iron constancy, add to his work schedule the continuous ill health he endured. He wrote to his physicians in 1564, when he was fifty-three years old, and described his colic and spitting of blood and ague and gout and the "excruciating sufferings" of his hemorrhoids.[4] But worst of all seemed to be the kidney stones that had to pass, unrelieved by any sedative.

> [They] gave me exquisite pain. . . . At length not without the most painful strainings I ejected a calculus which in

[2]Quoted in T. H. L. Parker, *John Calvin* (Philadelphia: Westminster Press, 1975), 104.
[3]Ibid., 103–4.
[4]John Dillenberger, *John Calvin, Selections from His Writings* (Atlanta: Scholars Press, 1975), 78.

some degree mitigated my sufferings, but such was its size that it lacerated the urinary canal and a copious discharge of blood followed. This hemorrhage could only be arrested by an injection of milk through a syringe.[5]

On top of all this pressure and physical suffering were the threats to his life. "He was not unfamiliar with the sound of mobs outside his house [in Geneva] threatening to throw him in the river and firing their muskets."[6] On his deathbed Calvin said to the pastors gathered, "I have lived here amid continual bickerings. I have been from derision saluted of an evening before my door with forty or fifty shots of an arquebus [a large gun]."[7] In a letter to Philipp Melanchthon in 1558, he wrote that war was imminent in the region and that enemy troops could reach Geneva within half an hour. "Whence you may conclude," he said, "that we have not only exile to fear, but that all the most cruel varieties of death are impending over us, for in the cause of religion they will set no bounds to their barbarity."[8] In other words, when he slept, he pondered from time to time what sorts of tortures would be inflicted on him if the armies entered Geneva.

Libertines and the Lord's Table

One of the most persistent thorns in Calvin's side was the libertines in Geneva. But here too his perseverance was

---

[5]Ibid.
[6]T. H. L. Parker, *Portrait of Calvin* (Philadelphia: Westminster Press, 1954), 29.
[7]Dillenberger, *John Calvin, Selections from His Writings*, 42.
[8]Ibid., 71.

triumphant in a remarkable way. In every city in Europe, men kept mistresses. When Calvin began his ministry in Geneva in 1536 at the age of twenty-seven, there was a law that said a man could keep only one mistress.[9] After Calvin had been preaching as pastor in St. Peter's church for over fifteen years, immorality was still a plague, even in the church. The libertines boasted in their license. For them, the "communion of saints" meant the common possession of goods, houses, *bodies*, and *wives*. So they practiced adultery and indulged in sexual promiscuity in the name of Christian freedom. And at the same time, they claimed the right to sit at the Lord's Table.[10]

The crisis of the Communion came to a head in 1553. A well-to-do libertine named Berthelier was forbidden by the Consistory of the church to eat the Lord's Supper but appealed the decision to the council of the city, which overturned the ruling. This created a crisis for Calvin who would not think of yielding to the state the rights of excommunication, nor of admitting a libertine to the Lord's Table.

The issue, as always, was the glory of Christ. He wrote to Viret:

> I . . . took an oath that I had resolved rather to meet death than profane so shamefully the Holy Supper of the Lord. . . . My ministry is abandoned if I suffer the authority of the Consistory to be trampled upon, and extend the Supper of Christ to open scoffers. . . . I should

---

[9]Parker, *Portrait of Calvin*, 29.
[10]Henry F. Henderson, *Calvin in His Letters* (London: J. M. Dent, 1909), 75.

rather die a hundred times than subject Christ to such foul mockery.[11]

The Lord's day of testing arrived. The libertines were present to eat the Lord's Supper. It was a critical moment for the Reformed faith in Geneva:

> The sermon had been preached, the prayers had been offered, and Calvin descended from the pulpit to take his place beside the elements at the communion table. The bread and wine were duly consecrated by him, and he was now ready to distribute them to the communicants. Then on a sudden a rush was begun by the troublers in Israel in the direction of the communion table. . . . Calvin flung his arms around the sacramental vessels as if to protect them from sacrilege, while his voice rang through the building: "These hands you may crush, these arms you may lop off, my life you may take, my blood is yours, you may shed it; but you shall never force me to give holy things to the profaned, and dishonor the table of my God."
>
> "After this," says Beza, Calvin's first biographer, "the sacred ordinance was celebrated with a profound silence, and under solemn awe in all present, as if the Deity Himself had been visible among them."[12]

Invincible Constancy

The point of mentioning all these woes in Geneva is to set in bold relief the invincible constancy of John Calvin in the ministry that God had called him to. We asked earlier, *What happened to John Calvin to make him a man so mastered*

---

[11]Ibid., 77.
[12]Ibid., 78–79.

by the majesty of God? And what kind of ministry did this produce in his life? We answered the first question by saying that Calvin experienced the supernatural, inward witness of the Spirit to the majesty of God in Scripture. From then on, everything in his thinking and writing and ministry was aimed at illustrating the majesty and glory of God.

Now, what is the answer to the second question—*what kind of ministry did his commitment to the majesty of God produce?* Part of the answer has been given: it produced a ministry of incredible steadfastness—a ministry, to use Calvin's own description of faithful ministers of the Word, of "invincible constancy."[13] But that is only half the answer. It was a ministry of unrelenting exposition of the Word of God. The constancy had a focus: the exposition of the Word of God, to which we turn in the next chapter.

---

[13]In a sermon on Job 33:1–7, Calvin calls preachers to constancy: "When men so forget themselves that they cannot subject themselves to Him Who has created and fashioned them, it behooves us to have an *invincible constancy*, and to reckon that we shall have enmity and displeasure when we do our duty; yet nevertheless let us go through it without bending." John Calvin, *Sermons from Job by John Calvin* (Grand Rapids, MI: Eerdmans, 1952), 245.

CHAPTER SEVEN

CONSTANCY IN EXPOUNDING THE WORD OF GOD

Calvin had seen the majesty of God in the Scriptures. This persuaded him that the Scriptures were the very Word of God. He said, "We owe to the Scripture the same reverence which we owe to God, because it has proceeded from Him alone, and has nothing of man mixed with it."[1] His own experience had taught him that "the highest proof of Scripture derives in general from the fact that God in person speaks in it."[2] These truths led to an inevitable conclusion for Calvin. Since the Scriptures are the very voice of God, and since they are therefore self-authenticating in revealing the majesty of God, and since the majesty and glory of God are the reason for all existence, it follows that Calvin's life would be marked by "invincible constancy" in the exposition of Scripture.

---

[1]Quoted in J. I. Packer, "Calvin the Theologian," in *Honouring the People of God: Collected Shorter Writings of J. I. Packer*, vol. 4 (Carlisle: Paternoster, 1999), 162. Calvin does not mean that there is not human agency in the inspiration of Scripture. His many commentaries bear witness to his careful attention to the human dimension of Scripture. He means that nothing human is mixed with God's intention in Scripture that would corrupt it.

[2]John Calvin, *Institutes of the Christian Religion*, 1.7.4.

Everything an Exposition of Scripture

He wrote tracts; he wrote the great *Institutes*; he wrote commentaries (on all the New Testament books except Revelation, plus the Old Testaments books of the Pentateuch, Joshua, Psalms, Isaiah, and Jeremiah); he gave biblical lectures (many of which were published as essentially commentaries); and he preached ten sermons every two weeks. But *all* of it was exposition of Scripture. John Dillenberger says, "[Calvin] assumed that his whole theological labor was the exposition of Scripture."[3] In his last will and testament, Calvin said, "I have endeavored, both in my sermons and also in my writings and commentaries, to preach the Word purely and chastely, and faithfully to interpret His sacred Scriptures."[4]

Everything was exposition of Scripture. This was the ministry unleashed by seeing the majesty of God in Scripture. The Scriptures were absolutely central because they were absolutely the Word of God and had as their self-authenticating theme the majesty and glory of God. But of all these labors of exposition, preaching was supreme. Emile Doumergue, the foremost biographer of John Calvin with his six-volume life of Calvin, said as he stood in the pulpit of John Calvin on the four hundredth anniversary of Calvin's birth, "That is the Calvin who seems to me to be the real and authentic Calvin, the one who explains all the others: Calvin the preacher of Geneva, molding

---

[3]John Dillenberger, *John Calvin, Selections from His Writings* (Atlanta: Scholars Press, 1975), 14.
[4]Ibid., 35ff.

by his words the spirit of the Reformed of the sixteenth century."[5]

Calvin's preaching was of one kind from beginning to end: he preached steadily through book after book of the Bible. He never wavered from this approach to preaching for almost twenty-five years of ministry in St. Peter's church of Geneva—with the exception of a few high festivals and special occasions.[6] "On Sunday he took always the New Testament, except for a few Psalms on Sunday afternoons. During the week . . . it was always the Old Testament."[7] The records show fewer than half a dozen exceptions for the sake of the Christian year. He almost entirely ignored Christmas and Easter in the selection of his text.[8]

The Scope of Calvin's Preaching

To give you some idea of the scope of Calvin's pulpit, he began his series on the book of Acts on August 25, 1549, and ended it in March of 1554. After Acts, he went on to the epistles to the Thessalonians (46 sermons), Corinthians (186 sermons), the Pastoral Epistles (86 sermons), Galatians (43 sermons), Ephesians (48 sermons)— until May of 1558. Then there is a gap when he was ill. In

---

[5]Quoted by Harold Dekker, in "Introduction," *Sermons from Job by John Calvin*, xii.
[6]Calvin's consistency is stunning at almost every level. J. I. Packer observes, "His consistency is remarkable. All that he wrote was homogeneous. He never changed his mind on any doctrinal issue. . . . 'Though he is of the number of those who grow old learning every day,' wrote Beza toward the end of Calvin's life, 'from the very beginning up to now, in all his many laborious writings, he has never set before the church one dogma about which he needed to alter his mind and part company with himself.'" J. I. Packer, "Calvin the Theologian," 144.
[7]T. H. L. Parker, *Portrait of Calvin* (Philadelphia: Westminster Press, 1954), 82.
[8]John Calvin, *The Deity of Christ and Other Sermons*, trans. Leroy Nixon (Grand Rapids, MI: Eerdmans, 1950), 8.

the spring of 1559, he began the harmony of the Gospels and was not finished when he died in May 1564. On the weekdays during that season, he preached 159 sermons on Job, 200 on Deuteronomy, 353 on Isaiah, 123 on Genesis, and so on.[9]

One of the clearest illustrations that this was a self-conscious choice on Calvin's part was the fact that on Easter Day of 1538, after preaching, he left the pulpit of St. Peter's, banished by the city council. He returned in September of 1541—over three years later—and picked up the exposition in the next verse.[10]

Why this remarkable commitment to the centrality of sequential expository preaching? Three reasons are just as valid today as they were in the sixteenth century.

First, *Calvin believed that the Word of God was a lamp that had been taken away from the churches.* He said in his personal testimony, "Thy word, which ought to have shone on all thy people like a lamp, was taken away, or at least suppressed as to us. . . . And now, O Lord, what remains to a wretch like me, but . . . earnestly to supplicate thee not to judge according to [my] deserts that fearful abandonment of thy word from which, in thy wondrous goodness thou hast at last delivered me."[11] Calvin reckoned that the continuous exposition of books of the Bible was the best way to overcome the "fearful abandonment of [God's] Word."

---

[9]For these statistics see Parker, *Portrait of Calvin*, 83, and W. de Greef, *The Writings of John Calvin: An Introductory Guide*, trans. Lyle D. Bierma (Grand Rapids, MI: Baker, 1993), 111–12.
[10]T. H. L. Parker, *Calvin's Preaching* (Louisville: Westminster, 1992), 60.
[11]Dillenberger, *John Calvin*, 115.

Second, T. H. L. Parker says that *Calvin had a horror of those who preached their own ideas in the pulpit.* He said, "When we enter the pulpit, it is not so that we may bring our own dreams and fancies with us."[12] He believed that by expounding the Scriptures as a whole, he would be forced to deal with all that *God* wanted to say, not just what *he* might want to say.

Third—and this brings us full circle to the beginning, where Calvin saw the majesty of God in his Word—*he believed with all his heart that the Word of God was indeed the Word of God, and that all of it was inspired and profitable and radiant with the light of the glory of God.* He challenged pastors of his day and ours:

> Let the pastors boldly dare all things *by the word of God.* . . . Let them constrain all the power, glory, and excellence of the world to give place to and to obey *the divine majesty of this word.* Let them enjoin everyone by it, from the highest to the lowest. Let them edify the body of Christ. Let them devastate Satan's reign. Let them pasture the sheep, kill the wolves, instruct and exhort the rebellious. Let them bind and loose thunder and lightning, if necessary, *but let them do all according to the word of God.*[13]

The Divine Majesty of the Word

The key phrase here is "the divine majesty of this word." This was always the root issue for Calvin. How might he best show forth for all of Geneva and all of Europe and all

---

[12]Parker, *Portrait of Calvin*, 83.
[13]John Calvin, *Sermons on the Epistle to the Ephesians* (Edinburgh: Banner of Truth, 1973), *xii*; emphasis added.

of history the majesty of God? He answered with a life of continuous expository preaching. There would be no better way to manifest the full range of the glories of God and the majesty of his being than to spread out the full range of God's Word in the context of the pastoral ministry of shepherding care.

This is why preaching remains a central event in the life of the church even five hundred years after the printing press and the arrival of radio and TV and computers. God's Word is mainly about the majesty of God and the glory of God. That is the main issue in ministry. And even though the glory and majesty of God in his Word can be known in the still, small voice of whispered counsel by the bedside of a dying saint, there is something in it that cries out for expository exultation. This is why preaching will never die. And radical, pervasive God-centeredness will always create a hunger for preaching in God's people. If God is "I AM WHO I AM"—the great, absolute, sovereign, mysterious, all-glorious God of majesty whom Calvin saw in Scripture—there will always be preaching, because the more this God is known and the more this God is central, the more we will feel that he must not just be analyzed and explained but acclaimed and heralded and magnified with expository exultation.

The flaming legacy of sovereign joy,[14] spread through centuries of fervent saints, is ignited anew in every genera-

---

[14]The phrase *sovereign joy* is unfolded in John Piper, *The Legacy of Sovereign Joy: God's Triumphant Grace in the Lives of Augustine, Luther, and Calvin* (Wheaton, IL: Crossway Books, 2006).

tion by glowing, God-besotted preaching—the preaching of the "divine majesty of this word." May God grant every preacher of the Word such a "taste" of sovereign joy in God and such an "intense desire" for him that expository exultation would flame up in every church.

CALVIN'S BARBARIC WORLD: THE CASE OF MICHAEL SERVETUS

The Europe that John Calvin was born into on July 10, 1509, was a harsh and immoral and even barbaric place to live. There was no sewer system or piped water supply or central heating or refrigeration or antibiotics or penicillin or aspirin or surgery for appendicitis or Novocain (for tooth extraction) or electric lights (for studying at night) or water heaters or washers or dryers or stoves or ballpoint pens or typewriters or computers or motors of any kind. Life was harsh.

Barbaric Times

Not only were the times harsh and immoral, they were often barbaric. This is important to see, because Calvin did not escape the influence of his times. He described in a letter the cruelty common in Geneva: "A conspiracy of men and women has lately been discovered who, for the space of three years, had [intentionally] spread the plague through the city, by what mischievous device I know not."

The upshot of this was that fifteen women were burned at the stake. "Some men," he said, "have even been punished more severely; some have committed suicide in prison, and while twenty-five are still kept prisoners, the conspirators do not cease . . . to smear the door-locks of the dwelling-houses with their poisonous ointment."[1]

This sort of punishment loomed on the horizon not just for criminals, but for all the Reformers. Calvin was driven out of his homeland of France under threat of death. For the next twenty years, he agonized over the martyrs there and corresponded with many of them. In 1552, five young pastors, who had been trained in Switzerland, returned as missionaries to France and were arrested. Calvin wrote to them through their trial. They were condemned to death by burning. "We pray," he wrote, "that [God] would glorify Himself more and more by your constancy, and that He may, by the comfort of His Spirit, sweeten and endear all that is bitter to the flesh, and so absorb your spirits in Himself, that in contemplating that heavenly crown, you may be ready without regret to leave all that belongs to this world."[2]

In a letter to Melanchthon on November 19, 1558, Calvin wrote that war was imminent in the region and that enemy troops could reach Geneva within half-an-hour. "Whence you may conclude," he said, "that we have not only exile to fear, but that all the most cruel varieties of death are impending over us, for in the cause of religion

[1]Henry F. Henderson, *Calvin in His Letters* (London: J. M. Dent, 1909), 63.
[2]T. H. L. Parker, *Portrait of Calvin* (Philadelphia: Westminster Press, 1954), 120.

they will set no bounds to their barbarity."[3] So Calvin lived in a time of incredible cruelty and almost daily vulnerability to death by agonizing disease or agonizing torture—and that without any hope of pain-relievers. It was a harsh and immoral and barbaric time.

The Best and Worst of Calvin

The atmosphere of the time gave rise to the greatest and the worst achievement of Calvin. The greatest was the writing of the *Institutes of the Christian Religion*, and the worst was his joining in the condemnation of the heretic Michael Servetus to burn at the stake in Geneva.

The *Institutes* was first published in March 1536, when Calvin was twenty-six years old. It went through five editions and enlargements until it reached its present form in the 1559 edition. If this is all Calvin had written—and not forty-eight volumes of other works—it would have established him as the foremost theologian of the Reformation. But it did not arise for merely academic reasons. Here's why he wrote it, soon after he had been driven from France and was safely hiding in Basel:

> But lo! whilst I lay hidden at Basel, and known only to few people, many faithful and holy persons were burnt alive in France. . . . It appeared to me, that unless I opposed them [the perpetrators] to the utmost of my ability, my silence could not be vindicated from the charge of cowardice and treachery. This was the consideration which induced me to

[3]John Dillenberger, *John Calvin, Selections from His Writings* (Atlanta: Scholars Press, 1975), 71.

publish my *Institutes of the Christian Religion*. . . . It was published with no other design than that men might know what was the faith held by those whom I saw basely and wickedly defamed.[4]

So it was the very barbarity of the times against the faithful in France that stirred up Calvin to write the first edition of the *Institutes*.

But it was this same barbarity from which he could not disentangle himself. Michael Servetus was a Spaniard, a medical doctor, a lawyer, and a theologian. His doctrine of the Trinity was unorthodox—so much so as to shock both Catholic and Protestant in his day. In 1553, he published his views and was arrested by the Catholics in France. But, alas, he escaped to Geneva. He was arrested there, and Calvin argued the case against him. He was sentenced to death. Calvin called for a swift execution, but he was burned at the stake on October 27, 1553.[5]

This has tarnished Calvin's name so severely that many cannot give his teaching a hearing. But it is not clear that most of us, given that milieu, would not have gone along under the circumstances.[6] Melanchthon was the gentle, soft-spoken associate of Martin Luther whom Calvin had met and loved. He wrote to Calvin on the Servetus affair, "I am wholly of your opinion and declare also that your magistrates acted quite justly in condemning the blasphemer to death."[7] Calvin

---

[4]Ibid., 27.
[5]Parker, *Portrait of Calvin*, 102.
[6]Parker describes some of those circumstances in *Portrait of Calvin*, 102.
[7]Henderson, *Calvin in His Letters*, 196.

never held civil office in Geneva[8] but exerted all his influence as a pastor. Yet, in this execution, his hands are as stained with Servetus's blood as David's were with Uriah's.[9]

Under the Banner of God's Mercy

The Servetus incident makes the confessions of Calvin near the end of his life all the more important. On April 25, 1564, a month before his death, he called the magistrates of the city to his room and spoke these words:

> With my whole soul I embrace the mercy which [God] has exercised towards me through Jesus Christ, atoning for my

---

[8]Benjamin Warfield, *Calvin and Augustine* (Philadelphia: Presbyterian and Reformed, 1971), 16.

[9]J. I. Packer tries to set the Servetus affair in the light of its time. "The anti-Trinitarian campaigner Servetus was burned at Geneva in 1553, and this is often seen as a blot on Calvin's reputation. But weigh these facts:

1) The belief that denial of the Trinity and/or Incarnation should be viewed as a capital crime in a Christian state was part of Calvin's and Geneva's medieval inheritance; Calvin did not invent it.

2) Anti-Trinitarian heretics were burned in other places besides Geneva in Calvin's time, and indeed later—two in England, for instance, as late as 1612.

3) The Roman Inquisition had already set a price on Servetus' head.

4) The decision to burn Servetus as a heretic was taken not only by Calvin personally but by Geneva's Little Council of twenty-five, acting on unanimous advice from the pastors of several neighboring Reformed churches whom they had consulted.

5) Calvin, whose role in Servetus' trial had been that of expert witness managing the prosecution, wanted Servetus not to die but to recant, and spent hours with him during and after the trial seeking to change his views.

6) When Servetus was sentenced to be burned alive, Calvin asked for beheading as a less painful alternative, but his request was denied.

7) The chief Reformers outside Geneva, including Bucer and the gentle Melanchthon, fully approved the execution.

The burning should thus be seen as the fault of a culture and an age rather than of one particular child of that culture and age. Calvin, for the record, showed more pastoral concern for Servetus than anyone else connected with the episode. As regards the rights and wrongs of what was done, the root question concerns the propriety of political paternalism in Christianity (that is, whether the Christian state, as distinct from the Christian church, should outlaw heresy or tolerate it), and it was Calvin's insistence that God alone is Lord of the conscience that was to begin displacing the medieval by the modern mind-set on this question soon after Servetus's death. The preceding is from Packer's essay "John Calvin and Reformed Europe," reprinted in *Honouring the People of God: Collected Shorter Writings of J. I. Packer*, vol. 4 (Carlisle: Paternoster Press, 1999), 18–19.

sins with the merits of his death and passion, that in this way he might satisfy for *all my crimes and faults,* and blot them from his remembrance. . . . I confess I have failed innumerable times to execute my office properly, and had not He, of His boundless goodness, assisted me, all that zeal had been fleeting and vain. . . . For all these reasons, I testify and declare that I trust to no other security for my salvation than this, and this only, viz., that as God is the Father of mercy, he will show himself such a Father to me, who acknowledge myself to be *a miserable sinner.*[10]

T. H. L. Parker wrote that Calvin "should never have fought the battle of faith with the world's weapons."[11] Whether Calvin came to that conclusion before he died, we don't know. But what we know is that Calvin knew himself "a miserable sinner" whose only hope in view of "all [his] crimes" was the mercy of God and the blood of Jesus.

So the times were harsh and immoral and barbaric and had a contaminating effect on everyone, just as we are all contaminated today by the evils of our time. Their blind spots and evils may be different from ours. And it may be that the very things they saw clearly are the things we are blind to. It would be foolhardy to say that we would have never done what they did under their circumstances, and thus draw the conclusion that they have nothing to teach us. In fact, what we probably need to say is that some of our evils are such that we are blind to them, just as they were blind to many of theirs, and the virtues they manifested in

---

[10]Dillenberger, *John Calvin,* 35; emphasis added.
[11]Parker, *Portrait of Calvin,* 103.

those times are the very ones that we probably need in ours. There was in the life and ministry of John Calvin a grand God-centeredness, Bible-allegiance, and iron constancy. Under the banner of God's mercy to miserable sinners, we would do well to listen and learn.

Desiring God
978-1-84474-0-444

Don't Waste your Life
978-1-84474-098-7

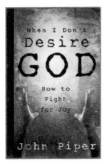

When I don't Desire God
978-1-84474-097-0

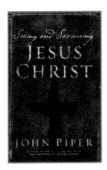

Seeing and Savouring Jesus Christ
978-1-84474-087-1

A Hunger for God
978-0-85111-193-3

Future Grace
978-0-85111-162-9

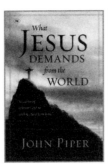

What Jesus Demands from the World
978-1-84474-171-7

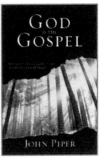

God is the Gospel
978-1-84474-109-0

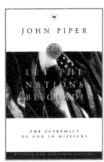

Let the Nations be Glad
978-0-85111-409-5

Amazing Grace in the Life of
William Wilberforce

Against great obstacles William Wilberforce fought for the abolition of the African slave trade and against slavery itself until they were both illegal in the British Empire.

Many are aware of Wilberforce's role in bringing an end to slavery in Great Britain, but few have taken the time to examine the beliefs and motivations that spurred him on for decades. In this concise volume, John Piper tells the story of how Wilberforce was transformed from an unbelieving, young politician into a radically God-centered Christian, and how his deep spirituality helped to change the moral outlook of a nation.

As world leaders debate over how to deal with a host of social justice and humanitarian crises, a closer look at Wilberforce's life and faith serves as an encouragement and example to all believers.

'John Piper's succinct and superbly perceptive study of William Wilberforce deserves to become an acclaimed bestseller. ... William Wilberforce's secret, as revealed in this book, was that he made the journey from self-centeredness, achievement-centeredness, and political-centeredness to God-centeredness. And he made it with Christlike joy.'

Jonathan Aitken

ISBN:
978-1-84474-185-4

Available from your local Christian bookshop or via our website at **www.ivpbooks.com**

www.ivpbooks.com

For more details of books published by IVP, visit our website where you will find all the latest information, including:

Book extracts   Downloads
Author interviews   Online bookshop
Reviews   Christian bookshop finder

You can also sign up for our regular email newsletters, which are tailored to your particular interests, and tell others what you think about this book by posting a review.

We publish a wide range of books on various subjects including:

Christian living   Small-group resources
Key reference works   Topical issues
Bible commentary series Theological studies

                www.ivpbooks.com